Remembering
Alexandria

Julie Ballin Patton and Rita Williams Holtz

TRADE PAPER
PRESS

Government Coal Wharf (ca. 1863).

Remembering
Alexandria

Turner Publishing Company
200 4th Avenue North • Suite 950
Nashville, Tennessee 37219
(615) 255-2665

Remembering Alexandria

www.turnerpublishing.com

Library of Congress Control Number: 2010924323

ISBN: 978-1-59652-666-2

Printed in the United States of America

10 11 12 13 14 15 16—0 9 8 7 6 5 4 3 2 1

CONTENTS

The 1971 T. C. Williams High School Varsity Football team, the Titans. The story of this team winning the state high school football championship was the basis for the movie *Remember the Titans*.

Acknowledgments

This volume, *Remembering Alexandria,* is the result of the cooperation and efforts of many individuals and organizations. It is with great thanks that we acknowledge the valuable contribution of the following for their generous support:

The Alexandria Library, Special Collections
The Library of Congress

The writers wish to thank George Combs, director of Alexandria Library, Special Collections, for allowing us the time to work on this book, and Michele Lee, Librarian at the Alexandria Library, Special Collections, for her extensive help in editing the manuscript. We also wish to thank the rest of the staff at Special Collections for their support during this project.

PREFACE

Alexandria has thousands of historic photographs that reside in archives, both locally and nationally. This book began with the observation that, while those photographs are of great interest to many, they are not easily accessible. During a time when Alexandria is looking ahead and evaluating its future course, many people are asking, How do we treat the past? These decisions affect every aspect of the city—architecture, public spaces, commerce, infrastructure—and these, in turn, affect the way that people live their lives. This book seeks to provide easy access to a valuable, objective look into the history of Alexandria.

The power of photographs is that they are less subjective than words in their treatment of history. Although the photographer can make subjective decisions regarding subject matter and how to capture and present it, photographs seldom interpret the past to the extent textual histories can. For this reason, photography is uniquely positioned to offer an original, untainted look at the past, allowing the viewer to learn for himself what the world was like a century or more ago.

This project represents countless hours of review and research. The researchers and writers have reviewed thousands of photographs in numerous archives. We greatly appreciate the generous assistance of the individuals and organizations listed in the acknowledgments of this work, without whom this project could not have been completed.

The goal in publishing this work is to provide broader access to this set of extraordinary photographs that seek to inspire, provide perspective, and evoke insight that might assist people who are responsible for determining Alexandria's future. In addition, the book seeks to preserve the past with adequate respect and reverence.

With the exception of touching up imperfections that have accrued with the passage of time and cropping where necessary, no changes have been made. The focus and clarity of many images are limited to the technology and the ability of the photographer at the time they were recorded.

The work is divided into eras. Beginning with some of the earliest known photographs of Alexandria, the first section records photographs from the Civil War era through the end of the nineteenth century. The second section spans the beginning of the twentieth century through World War I. Section Three covers the years between the wars, and the last section covers the World War II era to recent times. In each of these sections we have made an effort to capture various aspects of life through our selection of photographs. People, commerce, transportation, infrastructure, religious institutions, and educational institutions have been included to provide a broad perspective.

We encourage readers to reflect as they go walking in Alexandria, strolling through the city, its parks, and its neighborhoods. It is the publisher's hope that in utilizing this work, longtime residents will learn something new and that new residents will gain a perspective on where Alexandria has been, so that each can contribute to its future.

—*Todd Bottorff, Publisher*

Star Fire Company, located at 116 S. St. Asaph Street. The company changed its name to the Columbia Steam Fire Engine Company in 1871 (1867).

From Civil War to Century's End

(1860s–1899)

Colonel Elmer Ellsworth and James Jackson died at the Marshall House. When Ellsworth removed a Confederate flag from the roof, he was shot by Jackson, the proprietor, who in turn was killed by another Union soldier (May 24, 1861).

One of many stockades erected, this one was built along Union Street, to prevent Confederate sympathizers from sabotaging the buildings and docks along the waterfront held by the Union (ca. 1861).

The frigate *Pensacola* lies at anchor in Alexandria Harbor. A second-class steamer, weighing 2,158 tons, the *Pensacola* was built in Florida and completed at the Washington Navy Yard. She was a part of the naval fleet commanded by Admiral David G. Farragut (ca. 1861).

Union soldiers stand at attention outside the Slave Pen in the 1300 block of Duke Street (ca. 1862).

A woman stands beside the Slave
Pen located in the 1300 block of
Duke Street (ca. 1862).

The United States Military Railroad construction corps planes boards along the Alexandria waterfront (ca. 1862).

Military personnel inspect the trusses used to build railroad bridges (ca. 1862).

Officers of the First District Volunteers and civilians pose for the photographer in front of the City Hotel (ca. 1862).

The Forty-fourth New York Infantry encampment at the top of Shuter's Hill. This location gave occupying troops an unobstructed view of the Potomac River (ca. 1862).

Soldiers and civilians mill around Aspinwall Hall on the grounds of the Protestant Episcopal Theological Seminary (ca. 1862).

The Tide Lock of the Alexandria Canal during the Civil War. The lock was located between Montgomery and First streets (ca. 1862).

The headquarters of Captain J. G. C. Lee, army quartermaster, were located at the northeast corner of Princess and N. Fairfax streets (ca. 1862).

Built in 1812 to house the Mechanics Bank, this building in the 500 block of King Street became the office of the provost marshal for the Union Army (ca. 1862).

Samuel Heflebower, proprietor of the City Hotel, took the Oath of Allegiance (to the federal government) to stay in business during the Civil War. Citizens, Federal troops, and travelers took advantage of his being open, utilizing the bar in the back that kept Heflebower in business during this time (ca. 1862).

Union officers and soldiers lounge outside Aspinwall Hall on the grounds of the Protestant Episcopal Theological Seminary. One soldier appears to be standing guard (ca. 1863).

Boxcars sit on side tracks before the large United States Military Railroad engine house. Up to 60 engines could be stored in the huge building (ca. 1863).

The United States Steam Fire House was established and run by the U.S. Army quartermaster. The fire station was located on the south side of Princess Street between Lee and Fairfax streets (July 1863).

Military staff and visiting relief agents stand in front of the U.S. Sanitary Commission lodge. The commission was responsible for overseeing the care of the wounded and ill (ca. 1863).

This home, located near Fort Lyon, was used as headquarters for General Samuel P. Heintzelman (ca. 1863).

This three-story brick residence, located at 209 S. St. Asaph Street, was used by General John P. Slough, military governor of Alexandria, as his residence and headquarters. Beyond is the post office and the veterans' reserve headquarters (ca. 1863).

Sailors on board the Russian frigate *Osliaba* while making a port call at Alexandria (ca. 1863).

Battery Rodgers, located on the western shore of the Potomac River between Fairfax, Green, and Jefferson streets near Jones' Point. Erected in 1863, it provided protection from river attacks. The doors led to magazines where ammunition was stored (ca. 1863).

Battery Rodgers was originally named Battery Water. The name was changed to Rodgers in 1863 to honor Captain George W. Rodgers, U.S. Navy (April 15, 1864).

Magazines at Battery Rodgers for a Parrot (rifled) gun (1863).

General Samuel P. Heintzelman with a group of family and friends at Convalescent Camp (ca. 1863).

The remains of a train disabled by Confederate forces are readied for transport back to Alexandria (ca. 1863).

Camp Convalescent was located on the slope of Shuter's Hill. In this view, ambulances and buggy wait in front of the camp's entrance. Conditions inside were described as "squalid and horrible," earning the camp the nickname "Camp Misery" (ca. 1863).

The hub of the United States Military Railroad. Administration offices, the yards, and the roundhouse of what had been the Orange and Alexandria Railroad prior to the Civil War (ca. 1864).

A view of Alexandria from Fort Ellsworth. The Military Railroad and roundhouse are visible (April 1864).

This two-story, towered brick home at 508 Wolfe Street was used as a Union hospital from January 1862 through February 1865. The house is no longer standing.

This 15-inch Rodman gun was located at Battery Rodgers. Made of cast iron, the gun fired a 440-pound shot (May 18, 1864).

President Lincoln's railcar was built in government shops in Alexandria for his travel use. Before he was able to use the car, he was assassinated. The car was refitted to become the funeral car that took his body from Washington to Springfield, Illinois (1865).

A view from the six-story Pioneer Mill located on the south end of the waterfront. Ships of all sizes and shapes docked at Alexandria (May 1865).

Wooden markers designate the individual graves of Federal soldiers, both black and white, who are buried in the Alexandria National Cemetery. The wooden markers were later replaced with stone markers. There are nearly 3,600 interments (ca. 1865).

Cooks prepare food for convalescing soldiers in the kitchen at Soldier's Rest (July 1865).

A snowy King Street and the south side of the 400 and 500 blocks, facing west (ca. 1870).

A cobblestoned Cameron Street. Eastward is Christ Episcopal Church. The three-story brick home on the right at 607 Cameron was built in 1799 and is known as the Fairfax House. It was home to Lord Fairfax in 1830 (ca. 1880).

The Prince Street Wharf off the Strand (1883).

J. T. Creighton and Son Hardware, at 328 King Street, was one of Alexandria's longest-running businesses. Among the items advertised on this storefront are "Shovels, Plow Castings, Spades, Forks & Rakes."

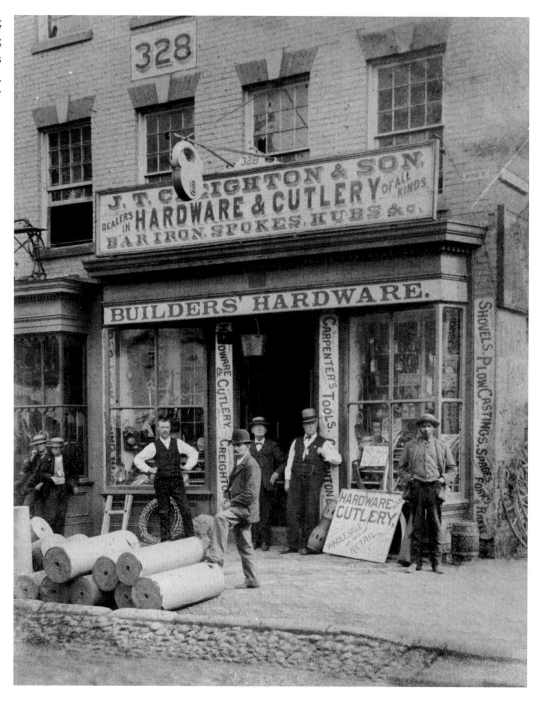

The old steam engine pumper inside Columbia Fire House Company No. 4 (ca. 1885).

At the corner of King and Peyton streets stood the Old Virginia House, in business since 1823. The hotel offered "large" bedrooms, dining rooms, a bar, and a parlor for travelers, and cost about a dollar a day. Damaged by fire and a tornado, it was razed around 1930 (ca. 1888).

King Street, facing east from the 700 block (ca. 1890s).

A street market in the 100 block of N. Royal Street (ca. 1895).

Alexandrians loved parades. Flags and bunting adorned buildings, and marching groups of every description participated in the parades of the nineteenth and early twentieth centuries. The sesquicentennial celebration shown in this 1899 image was no exception.

Banners and bunting festoon the drugstore owned by Edgar Warfield during the sesquicentennial parade in 1899.

Dressed in the latest fashion, a group of young women and two gentlemen pose playfully for the camera (ca. 1899).

The Post Office and Customs House, on the southwest corner of Prince and St. Asaph streets (ca. 1900).

A New Century and a World War

(1900–1919)

The former District Courthouse for Alexandria was located in the 300 block of N. Columbus Street. Designed by architect Robert Mills, the Greek Revival–style building and its grounds occupied the entire block. The building was demolished in 1905 (ca. 1900).

Ladies try their hand at "string and hook" fishing off one of the many piers on the waterfront. The gentleman is ready with net—if the fish bite! (ca. 1900).

All manner of debris created a never-ending cleaning job for the street cleaners of King Street (ca. 1900).

Once operated by John Gadsby, the City Hotel on Royal Street remained unchanged for many years. By 1900, there was a tavern in business on the lower level while the upper two floors were private living areas. Today the building houses Gadsby's Tavern and Museum.

A horse-drawn steam pumper stands in front of the Columbia Engine House no. 4 (ca. 1900).

The Alexandria Bicycle Club (ca. 1905).

The aftermath of a fire that destroyed the W. A. Smoot & Company planing mill and lumberyard (May 13, 1909).

Michelbach Furniture on King Street was one of Alexandria's leading retailers for many years. Here the building has been draped with bunting in preparation for one of the city's many parades (ca. 1910).

The surviving veterans of the Seventeenth Virginia Regiment proudly pose in front of 806 Prince Street, the Robert E. Lee Camp Hall. The group deeded the hall to the local chapter of the United Daughters of the Confederacy. It is now a museum honoring the men of the Seventeenth and the Confederacy (ca. 1910).

Horses were not the only means of pulling wagons. Here "Uncle Jack" guides the ox pulling his bare-bones wagon across Humes Spring. Mrs. Edith Snowdon looks on from the bank (ca. 1910).

Two large trees frame the home of Dr. M. M. Lewis on the corner of Cameron and N. Washington streets. This unusual photo was taken from the graveyard of Christ Episcopal Church (ca. 1910).

Shoe-shine stations along a busy Alexandria street (ca. 1910).

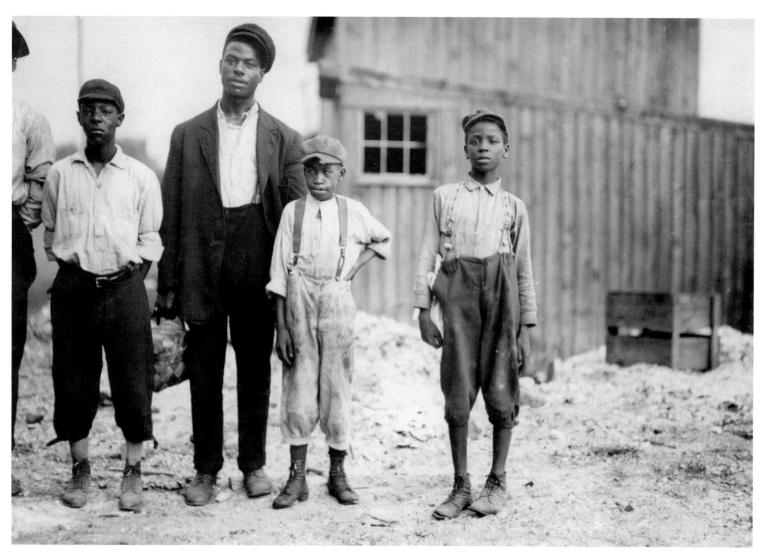

Before enactment of child labor laws, Alexandria glass factory workers included youths (June 1911).

The "carrying-in boy" at a glass factory. He took completed objects from the finisher to the tempering oven (June 1911).

When repairs to the cobblestone streets in Alexandria became too expensive, the stones were removed and stored at Cameron and Henry streets. Here a stone crusher breaks up the stones into gravel for road work (ca. 1912).

This panoramic view of the Virginia Ship Building Corporation shows offices and work areas. The company was located at the foot of Wolfe Street on the Potomac River and was in business for approximately 25 years (ca. 1918).

Joseph B. Drew's Saloon at 109 S. Pitt Street offered a summer garden where customers could sit outside and enjoy a drink. Wildfowl hang on the line in front of the establishment, ready to be plucked by the cook for the next meal (ca. 1915).

Fishing was not the only activity seen by this house and others like it, located north of Alexandria on Daingerfield Island.
Bootleggers and gamblers plied their trade here as did ladies of the evening (ca. 1910-15).

Alexandria soldiers went to Camp Humphries in Virginia during World War I. The arrangement of screens between beds was intended to prevent the spread of influenza (1918).

The Virginia Ship Building Corporation at the foot of Wolfe Street. Cranes, tracks, and scaffolding surround a vessel under construction (ca. 1915).

The front of Carlyle House, built in 1753 by John Carlyle. The house is located on Fairfax Street and is now a part of the Carlyle House Historic Park (ca. 1918).

The Confederate Monument, erected in 1889 to honor the fallen, stands at the intersection of Prince and Washington streets. This was the point from which soldiers left Alexandria at the beginning of the Civil War.

A horse-drawn pumper takes part in a parade (ca. 1920).

HARD TIMES AND ECONOMIC CHALLENGES

(1920–1939)

Washington and King streets (ca. 1920s).

The Alexandria Light Infantry Band in front of Armory Hall on Royal Street near Prince Street (ca. 1920).

Street clearing is under way on the 400 block of King Street after a severe snowstorm in 1922.

Men with shovels work hard to make King Street passable following the 1922 storm.

Alexandria Auto Supply Company at 104 S. Washington Street (ca. 1924).

President Calvin Coolidge (standing at right with top hat) and the First Lady attend the cornerstone-laying ceremony at the George Washington Masonic National Memorial (November 1, 1923).

Horses and wagons were still in use in Alexandria in 1924. This scene on King Street shows the blend of old and new.

Captain's Row, 100 block of Prince Street, in 1924. In earlier days, sea captains built their Federal-style homes close to the river and work. In 1827, both sides of the entire block were destroyed by fire, but most homes had been rebuilt by 1835.

This building at 515 N. Washington Street has a long history. Built in 1847, it was used as a cotton factory, a prison during the Civil War, a bottling factory for a brewery, and was later converted to manufacture spark plugs (ca. 1925).

Girls on roller skates pose in front of Wise's Tavern, built between 1777 and 1778 at 201 N. Fairfax. John Wise was proprietor from 1788 to 1792. Originally used as a tavern and stable, it was converted to two dwellings in the early nineteenth century. From 1916 to 1974, it served as the Anne Lee Memorial Home (1925).

Inside Warfield's Drug Store on King Street, one could order a Coca-Cola at the soda fountain (ca. 1925).

A garlanded old pumper provides a grand ride and parade entry. The Women's Auxiliary of the Alexandria Fire Department follows behind (ca. 1925).

The corner of King and Royal streets (ca. 1925).

Cohen's Clothing at 1104 King Street carried all the latest attire for the well-dressed man (ca. 1925).

King Street, the 400 block (ca. 1925).

King Street, the 600 block (ca. 1925).

Built before 1785, the Ramsay House is thought to be the oldest house in Alexandria. Once used to manufacture cigars, it was later a tavern called Ma's Place. Today it is the Alexandria Tourist Council and Visitors Center (1926).

Victorian-era storefronts grace the 400 block of King Street. The sign beneath the streetlight says "Parking Limit 1 Hour" (ca. 1926).

Prince Street Wharf. Cars are lined up waiting to board the ferry (1929).

The Potomac Company Canal. George Washington founded the Potomac Company in the 1770s and proposed establishing a canal along the Potomac to allow boats to skirt the most dangerous sections of the river. When Maryland, which had jurisdiction over the river, agreed to support the canal in 1784, Washington oversaw its initial construction. It was completed in 1802, after his death. In the 1820s, the Chesapeake and Ohio Canal company took control of the canal and operated it until 1899. Later, the Baltimore and Ohio Railroad owned it. Competition from the railroads eventually made the canal unprofitable and it ceased operations in 1924.

Alexandria City Hall and Market Place on Cameron and N. Royal streets. The original building was destroyed by fire in 1871. A new building was designed by Adolph Cluss and built by E. H. Delchay. The building housed a market house, courthouse, schoolhouse, two firehouses, and a jail, and today serves as City Hall (ca. 1930).

A parade in progress in 1930.

Wesley Snoots, one of the first officers to patrol by motorcycle for the Alexandria Police Department (ca. 1930s).

A rear view of the Carlyle House. The second-story porch and first-floor terrace were set atop the vaulted chambers used for storage (ca. 1930).

The men and vehicles of the Virginia Public Service Company on King Street (ca. 1930).

This statue of George Washington awaits installation inside the George Washington Masonic Memorial in 1950. The statue is 17 feet tall and weighs 7 tons.

Workers inside the Express Spark Plug Factory at 515 N. Washington Street (1930).

Gadsby's Tavern at 138 N. Royal Street (ca. 1930).

A George Washington birthday celebration in February 1930 along North Fairfax Street. The white-plumed group is the Richmond Light Infantry Blues.

The Alexandria Light Infantry on Royal Street (1930).

Memorial service for Confederate veterans. Colonel Edgar Warfield (center, in uniform) was the last surviving veteran (May 1932).

The Alexandria Light Infantry, Company I, in front of tents during summer camp at Virginia Beach (1932).

Members of the First Infantry during military exercises at the Armory. Left to right are Captain W. Cameron Roberts, Lieutenant W. Milton Glascow, Lieutenant John Arnold (ca. 1935).

Alexandria, Barcroft & Washington Transit Company buses provided transportation to the Hoover Airport (ca. 1935).

With bottles lining the shelves, these two gentlemen are ready to fill prescriptions at the Stabler-Leadbeater Apothecary Shop (ca. 1930).

Stabler-Leadbeater Drugs at King and S. Fairfax streets (ca. 1935).

An aerial view of King Street, facing west from the waterfront to the George Washington Masonic Memorial (ca. 1935).

A view of the George Washington Masonic Memorial across Hunting Creek (ca. 1935).

Corner of Prince and Washington streets. The Confederate Monument faces south. Behind the monument rises the U.S. Custom House and Post Office (1937).

The War Years and Postwar Prosperity

(1940–1970s)

Lipps' Cafe at 721 King Street in the 1940s. This was a popular place to get a meal, buy a magazine, or have coffee with friends.

An eighteenth-century re-enactment takes place in front of the Stabler-Leadbeater Apothecary Shop on S. Fairfax Street (ca. 1940).

The 1944 George Washington High School football team.

Assembling a torpedo at the Torpedo Factory (ca. 1943).

Torpedo Factory personnel during World War II. During the war, the factory ran 24 hours a day and produced torpedoes for both aircraft and submarines (ca. 1943).

As World War II servicemen, Alexandrians leave from the Union train station (May 12, 1943).

Mrs. Susie Glasgow promotes the sale of Christmas trees by the Optimist Club to benefit the local Boys Club (ca. 1945).

World War II servicemen wait to board the bus (June 1, 1945).

A view east from the George Washington Masonic Memorial toward downtown and the Potomac River (ca. 1945).

A view of the waterfront at the Old Dominion Boat Club dock during the Middle State Regatta (September 5, 1948).

Washington and King streets (ca. 1950).

Remember the Rams? The Alexandria Rams, shown here in 1951, were a semi-pro football team that integrated well before the famous T. C. Williams High School Varsity Titans. In 1964, they became the first integrated team ever to play in Charleston, South Carolina.

President Dwight D. Eisenhower and First Lady Mamie when they visited Christ Episcopal Church in February 1953.

A familiar landmark in Alexandria is the Washington Street United Methodist Church at 115 S. Washington Street. The cornerstone was laid in 1850. The church underwent extensive renovations in 1875 and 1899 (ca. 1955).

The 500 block of King Street in the 1960s.

The 400 block of King Street, in view here around 1970.

The Wilkes Street tunnel was built for the Orange & Alexandria Railroad in 1856 and is the only remaining structure of this early line. The tracks are now gone and it is used as a pedestrian walkway (1970).

The U.S. Coast Guard's *Eagle* calls on Alexandria during the annual waterfront festival (1977).

Notes on the Photographs

These notes, listed by page number, attempt to include all aspects known of the photographs. Each of the photographs is identified by the page number, a title or description, photographer and collection, archive, and call or box number when applicable. Although every attempt was made to collect all data, in some cases complete data may have been unavailable due to the age and condition of some of the photographs and records.